Cooking
with
Weed

Get baked with 35 recipes for hash inspired by Woodstock festival

Margie Stone

DOG 'n' BONE

Designer Geoff Borin
Editor Kate Reeves-Brown
Production manager Gordana Simakovic
Art director Sally Powell
Creative director Leslie Harrington
Illustrator @livelyscout

Published in 2024 by Dog 'n' Bone Books,
an imprint of Ryland Peters & Small Ltd
20–21 Jockey's Fields   341 E 116th St
London WC1R 4BW   New York, NY 10029

www.rylandpeters.com

10 9 8 7 6 5 4 3 2 1

A CIP catalog record for this book is available
from the US Library of Congress and the British
Library.

ISBN 978-1-912983-80-3

Printed in China

Contents

Get baked

They say that your wedding day or the days your children are born are the best ones of your life. And, sure, they were great days (shame my daughter has grown up to be somewhat of a Karen), but, if I'm going to be really honest, there were three days in the August of '69 that go down in history as the best days of my life. Between the 15th and 18th August, 1969, I lost myself and found myself on a dairy farm in Bethel, New York. Woodstock—the festival that rocked the world and defined my generation—was pure, unadulterated fun, love, harmony… and marijuana.

I'm not going to lie—I was high pretty much the whole time. As were most of the other half million people there. We smoked, we danced, we skinny-dipped, we laughed, we hugged… we *lived*. Over the years, I slowly transformed from that young, carefree hippie with flowers in her hair to a respectable teacher, to a PTA mom, to an empty nester, to who I am today: a silver-haired senior who has recently rediscovered her penchant for pot.

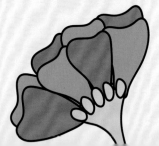

So, in the spirit of sharing, caring, and being daring, I have had a blast putting together this book, filled with my favorite cannabis-laced recipes that I hope will get you nicely buzzed. I have come up with five chapters: Boho Breakfasts & Brunches, Sky-High Snacks & Sharers, Dope Dinners, Sweeeeet Bakes, and Smokin' Smoothies & Hippy Shakes—reminiscing as I stir, chop, bake, and simmer, reliving my far-out, groovy, wonderful Woodstock days. I even tie-dyed my apron.

Peace.

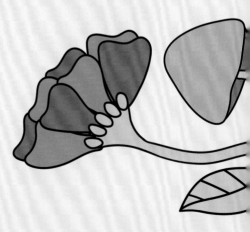

Why eat your weed?

Smoking pot is all very well and good, but by far the healthiest and most efficient way to absorb cannabinoids is to eat or drink them, which ensures that 100 percent of them enter your body. However, the rate of absorption is much slower than when inhaled, usually taking around 30-90 minutes to have an effect. The high also lasts considerably longer, with effects sometimes as long as 10 hours. If you are unsure of the potency, eat a small amount and wait a couple of hours before eating any more (gone are the days of the Woodstock "trip tents," where you could go if you were having a drug-induced wobble). If you do end up feeling a little too wonky, I suggest drinking the juice from fruits containing citric acid, such as orange or grapefruit, to reduce the effects. Eating pistachios or pine nuts can also help, as both contain pinene, a chemical that improves mental clarity.

Weed shouldn't just be eaten raw, as there are some properties that are brought on by heat. The THC present in raw weed is in its non-psychoactive form, tetrahydrocannabinolic acid (THCA). At 115-122°F (46-50°C), it begins releasing carbon dioxide and converts into its psychoactive form, tetrahydrocannabinol (THC). This reaction is known as decarboxylation, and it's pretty far out.

To be readily absorbed by the body, cannabinoids must first be dissolved. As they are lipophilic (can be dissolved in fats and oils), people usually extract the cannabinoids into butter, vegetable oil, or milk. These can be used, even when cold, to make cannabis-infused food and drink, known as "edibles."

The cannabinoids are also soluble in alcohol, so "tinctures" can be made by extracting cannabinoids into drinks with a high alcohol content. However, cannabinoids are insoluble in water. This is why brewing cannabis tea is not very effective unless the drink is combined with milk.

One final point: the serving quantities I've provided in this book are suggestions only and will vary depending on the strength of the cannabutter/oil/milk and your personal tolerance levels. Go easy at first, it's better to use too little than too much.

Right, now the scientific stuff is out of the way, allow me to take you on a journey back to 1969. Together, whilst we're making love not war, we'll also make brownies, dips, milkshakes, chicken, and more. It's time to eat, drink, and be merry!

How to make cannabutter and canna oil

The key ingredient to most cannabis-infused recipes is cannabutter or canna oil, which can even be made from the trimmings left over from harvest.

You will need:

2-4 oz (50-100 g) weed trimmings or 1-2 oz (25-50 g) buds, dried and ground (quantities can be varied to suit personal preference)

3 pints (1.5 liters) water

2 cups/4 sticks (450 g) butter or 2 pints (1 liter) vegetable oil

4 tbsp soy lecithin powder/granules (optional)

cheesecloth (muslin) and kitchen strainer (sieve)

2 large containers

Makes 16 oz (450 g) cannabutter or 2 pints (1 liter) canna oil

1 Before you make the cannabutter, the THC in the weed must undergo a process called decarboxylation (see page 6). To do this, preheat the oven to 220-240°F (104-116°C/gas mark 1). Keep the temperature within this range and never let it exceed 300°F (150°C/gas mark 2).

2 Spread the weed out on a baking sheet and cover loosely with foil, but seal it tightly around the edges of the baking sheet. Put into the oven for 30 minutes. Leave to cool fully before opening the foil, to prevent vapor loss.

3 Heat up the water in the pan, add the butter or oil and weed, stir, and bring to the boil. Reduce to a very low heat, put the lid on, and simmer for 2-3 hours, stirring occasionally.

4 Fold the cheesecloth (muslin) into a double layer, place in the strainer (sieve) and put that into a large container. Pour the mixture through.

5 Once all the liquid has drained through, bundle up the wet weed inside the cheesecloth and squeeze out as much remaining liquid as possible.

6 If using butter, put the container into the refrigerator. After a while, the water and butter will separate, with a layer of butter solidifying on top of the water. Once separated, discard the water. If using oil, leave the mixture out for 1-2 hours so the oil and water separate. Then put it in the freezer for 4-6 hours so the water freezes and you can pour off the oil. If the oil has coagulated in the freezer, scrape it off. It will liquefy at room temperature.

7 The butter or oil can be used as it is, but it can be further improved with the introduction of lecithin. When added, it will make the effects of the cannabis come on much faster and feel a lot stronger. Gently melt or warm the cannabutter or canna oil in a pan, stir in the lecithin until it dissolves, then pour the butter or oil back into the storage container. This will keep for about a month, or longer if frozen. Use it in place of some, or all, of the butter or oil in any recipes.

To make canna milk

Replace the butter or oil with milk and don't add water. As no water has been added, no subsequent separation is required.

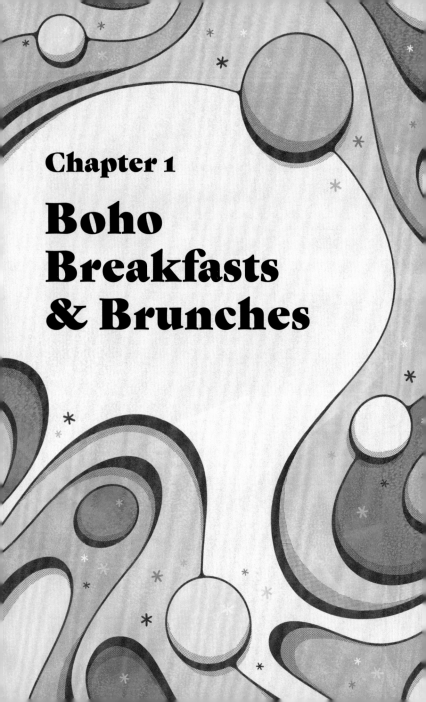

Chapter 1

Boho Breakfasts & Brunches

Yasgur's Yogurt

Hailed as "the man who hosted Woodstock," Max Yasgur offered up his 600-acre dairy farm as the location for the festival just a few weeks before it was scheduled to take place. Having been ousted from the original venue in the town of Woodstock, the organizers had to scramble to find an alternative, and came up trumps with Yasgur's "backyard," about 55 miles away in Bethel. Addressing the crowd, Yasgur said: "You've proven to the world that a half a million kids... can get together and have three days of fun and music and have nothing but fun and music, and God bless you for it!"

You will need:

1 tablespoon flavorless oil

2 pinches of hash, crumbled

2 small pots Greek-style yogurt

about 5 strawberries, hulled and quartered

about 20 blueberries or raspberries or a mixture of both

a squeeze of lemon juice

1 tablespoon runny honey or agave syrup, plus extra to drizzle

2 large handfuls of your favorite ready-made crunchy granola

Serves 2

1 Add the oil to a small skillet (frying pan). Crumble the hash into it, then gently heat to just infuse the oil with the hash, but don't let it catch and burn. Set aside to cool .

2 Tip the yogurts into a small mixing bowl. Stir in the cooled hash-infused oil.

3 Put the berries in a separate bowl and add a squeeze of lemon juice and a little honey or agave syrup to sweeten. Stir to coat the fruit in the liquid.

4 Take 2 straight-sided glasses or clear tumblers. Add a layer of granola to each, followed by a layer of the yogurt mixture, and a layer of the fruit mixture. Repeat to create 6 layers.

5 Finish with a sprinkle of the granola and a drizzle of honey or agave. Serve at once.

Flour Power Pancakes

You'll flip over these panache-packed pancakes. You'd have flipped over my attire in my youth too: floaty dresses with blooms embroidered on, tie-dye flares, fringe vests, and, most importantly, flowers in my hair. After I'd finished making these pancakes, I walked past the mirror in my hallway and noticed that I had *flour* in my hair. How times have changed. Sigh. I think on my next hike in the mountains, I'll pick some wildflowers to fashion myself a new headdress.

You will need:

1½ cups (250 g) all-purpose (plain) flour

2 teaspoons baking powder

3 tablespoons white granulated sugar

1 teaspoon salt

a small pinch of sweet ground cinnamon

2 eggs

1 cup (250 ml) full-fat (whole) milk

4 tablespoons cannabutter (see page 8), melted, plus an extra pat (knob) for cooking

To serve:

4 bananas, halved lengthwise

about 4 tablespoons dulce de leche, or other caramel sauce, to drizzle

Makes about 10 pancakes

1 Place the flour, baking powder, sugar, salt, and cinnamon in a large mixing bowl.

2 Lightly beat the eggs and milk together in a pitcher (jug) and add the melted cannabutter to this wet mixture.

3 Pour the wet mixture into the dry ingredients and stir to combine and make a loose batter.

4 Preheat a heavy-based skillet (frying pan) until very hot.

5 Add a pat (knob) of cannabutter to the skillet. Pour in about 3 tablespoons of the pancake batter to create your first pancake. Fry on one side, and then flip over using a large spatula and cook the other side until golden. Repeat until all the batter has been used. (Keep the pancakes warm as you go by stacking them on a plate and covering with a clean kitchen cloth.)

6 When the pancakes are all cooked, add the bananas to the same skillet and cook for 3-4 minutes, turning once, until lightly browned.

7 To serve, stack the pancakes on plates, top with the fried bananas and add a drizzle of dulce de leche. Enjoy warm.

Second-Time Cinnamon Loaf

"This is the second time we've ever sung in front of people, man. We're scared shitless!" So announced Stephen Stills—of Crosby, Stills & Nash—who had just played their first-ever gig the night before Woodstock at the Auditorium Theater in Chicago. And, right before our eyes, a few songs into their set—much to the audience's excitement—the supergroup became Crosby, Stills, Nash & Young, when Neil Young stepped onto the stage to perform "Mr Soul." As soon as I saw Mr Young, I couldn't help but recall the song "Cinnamon Girl," one of my favorites of his. I hope my Second-Time Cinnamon Loaf becomes a favorite of yours.

You will need:

2 cups (230 g) all-purpose (plain) flour

1 cup (225 g) soft brown sugar

2 teaspoons baking powder

½ teaspoon baking soda (bicarbonate of soda)

1½ teaspoons ground sweet cinnamon

½ teaspoon salt

1 cup (240 ml) buttermilk

¼ cup (60 ml) vegetable oil

2 eggs

1 teaspoon cardamom extract (optional)

2 teaspoons unsalted butter, softened

4 teaspoons cannabutter, softened (see page 8)

Vanilla glaze:

1 cup (115 g) confectioners' sugar (icing sugar)

2 tablespoons unsalted butter, melted and cooled slightly

½ teaspoon vanilla extract

¼ teaspoon salt

3–4 tablespoons milk, as needed

a 9 x 5 x 3-inch (23 x 13 x 7-cm) loaf pan, greased and lined with baking parchment

Makes 1 loaf

1 Preheat the oven to 350°F (180°C) gas 4.

2 Place the flour, sugar, baking powder, baking soda (bicarbonate of soda), cinnamon, salt, buttermilk, vegetable oil, eggs, cardamom extract (if using), butter and cannabutter in a mixing bowl.

3 Use a handheld electric whisk to beat the mixture vigorously for about 3 minutes until everything is combined.

4 Spoon the mixture into the greased and lined loaf pan. Use a spatula to level the top of the mixture.

5 Bake the loaf in the preheated oven for 45–50 minutes, until a skewer pushed into the center comes out clean.

6 Remove from the oven and leave to cool in the pan.

7 When the loaf is cool, make the vanilla glaze. Sift the confectioners' sugar (icing sugar) into a mixing bowl and then add the other ingredients. Stir until combined, loosening with a splash more milk as necessary to achieve a liquid consistency.

8 Use the tines of a fork to drizzle the glaze in a zig zag pattern over the top of the loaf. Allow to set before lifting the loaf out the pan and cutting into slices to serve.

Volkswagen Veggie Brekkie

My best friend Mary and I hitched a ride in a VW campervan, driven by a kind-eyed guy called David. There were nine of us crammed in there. En route, we sang, laughed, and discussed our protests against the Vietnam War. Inside the festival, parked by the main stage, was the now-famous Light Bus— the ultimate hippie mobile. Adorned with wings, hearts, stars, and other symbols of peace, love, and the universe's energy, how I wish I'd stuck my head in and introduced myself to Light, the band from Baltimore to whom it belonged.

You will need:

1 tablespoon vegetable oil

4 tablespoons cannabutter (see page 8)

10-12 medium white button mushrooms, quartered

a few large pieces of lemon peel plus ½ a lemon for squeezing

1 dried bay leaf

a pinch of dried oregano

1 garlic clove, peeled and flattened with a knife

a splash of white wine

salt and black pepper

To serve:

toasted sourdough bread

cream cheese (optional)

Serves 1–2

1 Heat the oil and cannabutter in a skillet (frying pan) until the butter has melted. Add the mushrooms, lemon peel, bay leaf, oregano, garlic, and white wine and cook for about 5-8 minutes, stirring, until the mushrooms are soft.

2 Remove from the heat. Remove the lemon peel, bay leaf, and garlic clove and set aside. Season the mushrooms generously with salt and pepper.

3 Spoon onto toasted sourdough bread (spread thickly with cream cheese, if you like) and serve immediately.

Bumper-to-Bumper Beans

Every traffic jam I've been in since Woodstock pales in comparison. Vehicles snarled up for 17 miles meant that many revelers—including me and my buddies—had to abandon ship (or VW) and walk miles and miles to reach the festival. The freeway basically turned into a parking lot! How I wish we'd thought to pack food—a hearty helping of these beans would have been the perfect antidote to my sore feet.

You will need:

1 tablespoon olive oil

a pat (knob) of unsalted butter

1 white onion, finely chopped

1 garlic clove, minced

a pinch of hot smoked paprika

1 tablespoon tomato paste (purée)

⅛ cup (8 g) hash, crumbled

1 x 14-oz (400-g) can chopped Italian tomatoes

1 teaspoon red wine vinegar

2 x 14-oz (400-g) cans cannellini beans, drained and rinsed

salt and black pepper

To serve:

fried or poached eggs (optional)

freshly chopped flat-leaf parsley

French stick (baguette), sliced

Serves 4

1 Heat the olive oil and butter in a skillet (frying pan) over a low heat until the butter has melted. Add the onion and garlic and sauté for about 5 minutes until the onion has softened, but take care not to burn the garlic.

2 Add the paprika and tomato paste (purée) and crumble in the hash. Mix together into a paste before adding the canned tomatoes and vinegar. Cook gently for 5–10 minutes.

3 Add the cannellini beans and cook gently for 5 minutes to heat through. Season with salt and pepper.

4 Spoon into shallow serving bowls, top with a fried or poached egg, if liked, and sprinkle over some chopped parsley. Serve warm with bread for mopping up the sauce.

Chapter 2

Sky-High Snacks & Sharers

No-Show Nachos

The Beatles, Led Zeppelin, Bob Dylan, The Doors, The Jeff Beck Group, Joni Mitchell, The Rolling Stones, The Moody Blues... I didn't see any of these at Woodstock because, for varying reasons, they all declined the invitation to play. Some didn't want to hang out with hippies in the mud, some broke up on the eve of the festival and some, like Tommy James and the Shondells, had been mis-sold, being told by their secretary: "There's this pig farmer in upstate New York that wants you to play in his field." Kicking themselves, much?

You will need:

7 oz (200 g) large plain tortilla chips

2 large tomatoes, deseeded and roughly chopped

4 tablespoons corn (sweetcorn) kernels, fresh or frozen

1 cup (250 g) grated firm mozzarella

3 tablespoons sliced jalapenos from a jar, drained, plus extra to garnish

¼ cup (12 g) hash, crumbled

black pepper

Toppings:

sour cream

guacamole (optional, see page 20)

freshly chopped cilantro (coriander)

paprika

Serves 6

1 Preheat the oven to 400°F (200°C) gas 6.

2 Arrange the tortilla chips in a single layer in a baking dish. Top with the chopped tomatoes, corn (sweetcorn) kernels, and grated cheese. Scatter the sliced jalapenos and hash over the top and season generously with black pepper.

3 Bake in the oven for 5–8 minutes until the cheese has melted and is bubbling.

4 Top with dollops of sour cream and guacamole (if using), and sprinkle over the chopped cilantro (coriander) and a few extra jalapenos. Dust with paprika and serve immediately while the cheese is still molten.

Hippy Dippies

Don't let the man keep you down... Make love, not war... Drop acid, not bombs... Boy, did I love being part of the hippy movement. My parents—God rest their souls—didn't get it. They were constantly scratching their heads and raising their eyebrows at me. But one thing we did agree on was dips. Clam dip, onion dip, bean dip, and, indeed, avocado dip and tomato salsa—we loved them all. Not sure they'd have approved of the extra herby addition to these ones though.

Guacamole:

3 ripe avocados, halved and pitted

1 ripe tomato, chopped

1 small red onion, finely chopped

1 chili, deseeded and finely chopped

a handful of freshly chopped cilantro (coriander)

juice of 1 lime

2 tablespoons canna oil (see page 8)

salt and black pepper

Serves 6-8

1 Scoop out the flesh of the avocados into a bowl, then add the tomato, onion, chili and cilantro (coriander). Add the lime juice and canna oil, and season with salt and pepper.

2 Use a fork to mash it all up until it gets to your preferred consistency.

Salsa:

4 ripe tomatoes, chopped

¼ red onion, chopped

¼ red bell pepper, chopped

a handful of freshly chopped cilantro (coriander)

3 garlic cloves, minced

1 jalapeño pepper, finely chopped

juice of 1 lime

4 tablespoons canna oil (see page 8)

salt and black pepper

Serves 4

1 Mix all the ingredients in a bowl and season with salt and pepper.

2 Toss thoroughly and leave to stand for 30 minutes before serving.

Tzatziki Skinny Dip

At Woodstock, you left your inhibitions at the gate. Many of us let it all hang out as we disrobed and dove into Filippini Pond, which was more of a lake really. Caked in mud after the rainstorms, it was the only way we could get clean. And it was SO fun! I wanted to create a dip to remember my bare-breasted bravery, and tzatziki seemed the obvious choice because, well, I saw plenty of "cucumbers" in that body of water!

You will need:

1 cucumber

about 2 cups (450 g) Greek-style yogurt

1 tablespoon lemon juice

2 garlic cloves, minced

½ cup (30 g) marijuana, finely chopped

1 tablespoon freshly chopped mint

salt and black pepper

To serve:

a selection of raw vegetable crudités and bread sticks

Serves 6–8

1 Cut the cucumber in half lengthwise and use a teaspoon to scoop out the seeds. Grate the cucumber flesh on a box grater directly into a mixing bowl.

2 Add the yogurt to the grated cucumber, along with the lemon juice, garlic, marijuana and chopped mint. Season generously with salt and pepper.

3 Transfer it to a shallow serving dish, cover and refrigerate for at least 1 hour before serving. This will allow the flavors to develop.

4 Serve with crudités, such as carrot batons and cauliflower florets, and bread sticks.

Freebie Falafels

I would have happily paid to go to Woodstock—it would have been worth every penny—but it turned out that I didn't need to. The sea of people arriving (many a couple of days before the festival even began) meant that fencing, entrance gates and ticket booths weren't set up yet. The logistics of doing this proved too much and the organizers thought, "To hell with it—let's make Woodstock a freebie!"

You will need:

1 tablespoon olive oil

1 white onion, finely chopped

2 garlic cloves, minced

1 teaspoon ground cumin

1 teaspoon ground coriander

3 cups (675 g) canned garbanzo beans (chickpeas), drained and rinsed

2 cups (450 g) cooked fava (broad) beans (you can buy these frozen; simply boil and squeeze the out of the skins before using)

1 cup (60 g) marijuana, finely chopped

salt and black pepper

all-purpose (plain) flour, for dusting

about 2-3 tablespoons vegetable oil, for frying

To serve (optional):

warmed pita breads

crisp mixed salad (iceberg lettuce, tomatoes, cucumber)

hummus

Serves 8

1 Add the olive oil to a skillet (frying pan). Sauté the onion, garlic, cumin, and coriander until the onion and garlic are soft and very slightly browned.

2 Purée the garbanzo beans (chickpeas) and skinned fava (broad) beans in a blender. Scrape the bean purée into a mixing bowl and tip in the onion mixture.

3 Stir in the marijuana and season generously with salt and black pepper.

4 Cover the bowl and leave the falafel mixture to stand in a cool place for about 30 minutes until the mixture is firm.

5 Use your hands to work the mixture into small round patties. Dip each one in the flour to dust lightly.

6 Heat the vegetable oil in the skillet (frying pan), and shallow fry the falafel patties, turning once, until golden brown on both sides and cooked through.

7 Serve immediately in warmed pita breads with salad and hummus for a substantial sandwich, or just dip into either of the dips on pages 20-21 to enjoy as a snack!

Bindy Bazaar Garlic Bread

I loved wandering through Bindy Bazaar, the wooded area set away from the main field, complete with trails, craft stalls, and a couple of tire swings. I got myself a trinket from a friendly vendor... then swiftly lost it whilst swinging on said tire swing. Oops! The trails included Gentle Path, Groovy Way, and High Way. Crunch your way through this garlic and parsley bread and you'll be on your very own "high way" in no time.

You will need:

2 garlic cloves, minced

2 teaspoons cannabutter, softened (see page 8)

2 tablespoons salted butter, softened

2 tablespoons freshly chopped flat-leaf parsley

1 part-baked French stick (baguette), halved lengthwise

Makes 1

1 Preheat the oven to 350°F (180°C) Gas 4.

2 Put the minced garlic and cannabutter in a bowl. Add the regular butter and the chopped parsley. Use a spoon to mix it all together until thoroughly combined.

3 Spread the butter mixture on the cut side of one of the French stick (baguette) halves, then press the two halves back together.

4 Wrap the bread in foil and put it in the oven, directly on the oven shelf, and bake for 10 minutes.

5 Remove from the oven, open the foil, slice using a bread knife, and serve immediately.

Santana Salmon

Santana owes its still-going career to Woodstock. They exploded onto the stage with one of the best drum solos in rock history and "Soul Sacrifice" became an anthem for the festival. As I danced to their Latin beats and marveled at their energy on stage, I started to wonder if perhaps their minds were... elsewhere. Sure enough, I later learned they were off their heads on the psychedelic mescaline. Guitarist Carlos Santana thought his guitar had transformed into a snake! Eating snake doesn't sound too appealing to me, so I opted for salmon for this recipe.

You will need:

2 tablespoons Dijon mustard

1 tablespoon superfine (caster) sugar

1 very fresh egg yolk

1 cup (240 ml) groundnut oil

4 tablespoons freshly chopped dill

a sprinkle of finely chopped marijuana (add more for a stronger effect)

1 tablespoon white wine vinegar

4–6 slices dark rye bread

1 large packet smoked salmon or smoked trout

salt and black pepper

finely sliced radishes, to garnish (optional)

Serves 4–6

1 In a mixing bowl, whisk the mustard and sugar together with the egg yolk. Slowly whisk in a steady trickle of groundnut oil, making sure the oil is well emulsified and you have a mayonnaise-like consistency.

2 Add the chopped dill, marijuana, and vinegar, and stir well to combine. Season generously with salt and pepper.

3 Lay out 4–6 slices of rye bread on a platter and top each one with a few slices of smoked salmon or trout. Spoon over the sauce and top with a few slices of radish to garnish (if using). Serve immediately.

Dreamy Honey Pecan Popcorn

Because hard-rock band Mountain whipped the crowd into such a state of exhilaration with their "Dreams of Milk and Honey" number, I thought I'd whip up some honey popcorn in their honor. Milk and honey combined is said to represent completeness, harmony, and pleasure... and as the song climaxed with an extended guitar solo, I felt all of these things in abundance. Serve this sweet snack with milk for the full Mountain-munching experience.

You will need:

2 tablespoons vegetable oil

7 oz (200 g) popcorn kernels

4 oz (125 g) cannabutter, diced (see page 8)

¾ cup (150 g) superfine (caster) sugar

2 tablespoons runny honey

¾ cup (100 g) chopped pecans

Serves 2-4

1 In a large pan, heat the vegetable oil and add the popcorn kernels. Put a lid on the pan and cook for 3-4 minutes until the popping stops, shaking the pan occasionally. Transfer to a large bowl.

2 Wipe the pan clean with a cloth. Add the cannabutter to the pan, along with the sugar and honey. Heat gently, stirring all the time, until the sugar has completely dissolved.

3 Bring to the boil and bubble rapidly, without stirring, for 4-5 minutes. The mixture will be ready when it has turned a caramel color.

4 Add the popcorn and chopped pecans and thoroughly stir until all the popcorn is coated in caramel and nuts.

5 Empty the pan onto a couple of non-stick baking sheets and leave to cool. Once cooled and hardened, break up into pieces and serve in a bowl.

Hendrix Hash Balls

I stayed until the bitter end of the festival, of course. I think these days they'd call that FOMO. I was exhausted, filthy, and ready to sleep for a week, but as I swayed along to the final act—the legend that was Jimi Hendrix—I felt a burst of rejuvenation. And when he let riff on his guitar with "The Star-Spangled Banner," well, I thought I might just be able to go on partying for three more days.

You will need:

2 cups (450 g) roasted cashew nut butter

a handful of dried goji berries

2 cups (230 g) finely shredded dried coconut, plus extra to coat

½ cup (55 g) ground almonds

1 cup (60 g) pulverized cannabis (use a pestle and mortar to do this)

3-4 tablespoons maple syrup

a baking sheet, lined with baking parchment

Makes 20-30 balls (depending on size)

1 Put all the ingredients into a mixing bowl and knead together until well combined.

2 Tip the mixture out onto a clean work surface and use a rolling pin to roll it out into a rectangle about 2 inches (4 cm) thick. Using a knife, cut the rectangle into as many bite-sized pieces as you can. Use your hands to roll each piece in a small ball and put them on the lined baking sheet.

3 Sprinkle extra shredded coconut onto a plate and roll each ball in it to coat lightly.

4 Put the coconut-coated balls on a clean plate and leave to chill in the refrigerator overnight.

5 Remove from the fridge just before serving to allow them to soften slightly.

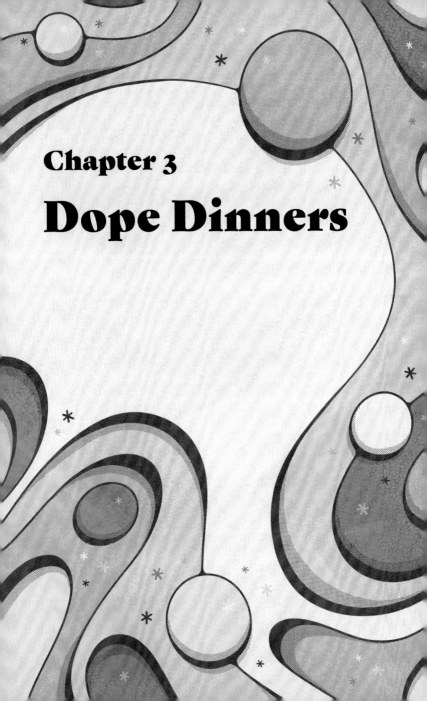

Chapter 3
Dope Dinners

Shockingly Good Steak

Although The Grateful Dead have been described as "legendary," "iconic," and "the greatest American rock band of all time," their Woodstock performance was kind of a bummer and they only played five songs. Drummer Mickey Hart later said, "It was a very terrible moment for us. The stage was collapsing. It was raining. Jerry [Garcia] and Bob [Weir] were getting shocked at the microphones." So, in order to counter the band's shockingly bad Woodstock set, I give you this Shockingly Good Steak.

You will need:

4½ oz (120 g) cannabutter, softened (see page 8)

4 oz (100 g) soft blue cheese

1 tablespoon snipped chives

1 teaspoon olive oil

4 fillet steaks

black pepper

To serve:

arugula (rocket) and

fries (chips)

Serves 4

1 Put the softened cannabutter in a mixing bowl. Crumble in the blue cheese and use a small spatula or wooden spoon to mix until combined. Add the chives and work into the butter.

2 Spoon the butter onto a sheet of baking parchment and shape into a roll. Use the paper to roll the butter into a cylinder with a diameter of about 2 inches (4 cm). Twist the ends to secure tightly and then wrap the whole thing in plastic wrap (cling film), rolling on the work surface to maintain the cylindrical shape.

3 Put in the fridge to chill and firm up for a least 2 hours. When ready to use, remove from the fridge and use a sharp knife to slice into rounds about 1 inch (1 cm) thick.

4 Heat the oil in a heavy-based skillet (frying pan). Add the steaks and cook to your taste. Plate the hot steaks and top each one with a round of the chilled butter so that it melts.

5 Add a generous handful of arugula (rocket) and some hot fries (chips) to the plate for a delicious dinner.

Pizza, Love & Understanding

Time magazine described Woodstock as "the greatest peaceful event in history." And I can attest to that. Never before had I felt such unity, freedom, warmth and inspiration... and I've never had the same feeling since. Richie Havens, who opened the festival, said: "Woodstock was not about sex, drugs, and rock and roll. It was about spirituality, about love, about sharing, about helping each other, living in peace and harmony." Share the love as you share this pizza, each piece bringing a slice of hope into your life.

You will need:

10 fl oz (300 ml) warm water

1 sachet fast-action dried yeast

1 tablespoon sugar

3 tablespoons canna oil (see page 8), plus extra for drizzling

3 cups (375 g) all-purpose (plain) flour, plus extra for dusting

1 teaspoon dried thyme

1 teaspoon salt

2 handfuls grated firm mozzarella

your favorite toppings (optional)

For the sauce:

1 x 14-oz (400-g) can chopped plum tomatoes

3 tablespoons tomato paste (purée)

3½ fl oz (100 ml) canna oil (see page 8)

2 garlic cloves, minced

½ tablespoon dried basil

½ tablespoon dried oregano

½ tablespoon chili powder

salt and black pepper

Makes 2

1 Put all the sauce ingredients into a pan with ½ teaspoon each of salt and pepper. Cook over a medium heat, stirring well. Bring to a gentle boil, then lower the heat and simmer for 30 minutes, stirring occasionally. Remove from the heat, transfer to a bowl, and refrigerate for a couple hours.

2 To make the pizza base, mix the water, yeast, sugar, and oil in a bowl. Add the flour, thyme, and salt. Mix and knead for 10–12 minutes, sprinkling with flour to stop it sticking to the bowl.

3 The dough should be elastic and smooth. Place it in an oiled bowl, drizzle with some more oil, cover with plastic wrap (cling film), and let stand for an hour.

4 Separate the dough into two halves and roll them into balls. Cover with a damp dish towel and leave to stand for another 10 minutes. Preheat the oven to 400°F (200°C/ gas 6).

5 Roll the dough out onto two pizza pans or stones and poke some holes in it with a fork to let steam escape while cooking. Now all that's left is to smother your pizza bases with the special tomato sauce, sprinkle on some grated mozzarella cheese and add any of your favorite toppings, if you like.

6 Bake in the oven for about 20 minutes, then serve.

Baez Bolognese

When I was six months pregnant, it was all I could do to waddle around the house eating ice cream, but Joan Baez got on stage and performed her socks off. I just loved watching the folk singer/political activist—who had been to jail for her protests against the Vietnam War—belt out "Oh Happy Day" and "Swing Low, Sweet Chariot." But when she sang "We Shall Overcome" (which she had performed at the 1963 March on Washington when Martin Luther King momentously declared "I have a dream"): goosebumps.

You will need:

2 tablespoons olive oil

3 lb (1.25 kg) ground (minced) lean turkey

2 white onions, roughly chopped

3 garlic cloves, minced

2 glasses fruity red wine

2 chicken or vegetable bouillon (stock) cubes

2 x 14-oz (400-g) cans Italian chopped tomatoes

2 tablespoons sun-dried tomato paste (purée)

4 oz (125 g) field mushrooms, sliced

2 dried bay leaves

1 teaspoon dried oregano

½ cup (30 g) marijuana, finely chopped

a splash of Worcestershire sauce (optional)

1 tablespoon freshly chopped basil

salt and black pepper

To serve:

1 packet dried spaghetti

finely grated Parmesan cheese

Serves 6–8

1 Heat the olive oil in a large saucepan set over a medium heat, add the ground (minced) turkey and sauté until lightly browned.

2 Add the chopped onions and minced garlic, and fry until the onions have softened.

3 Pour in the red wine and crumble in the bouillon (stock) cubes. Boil, uncovered, until the liquid has reduced in volume by about one-third.

4 Reduce the temperature to low. Stir in the canned tomatoes, sun-dried tomato paste (purée), mushrooms, bay leaves, oregano, marijuana, and Worcestershire sauce (if using). Season generously with salt and pepper.

5 Cover the saucepan with a lid and simmer for about 45–60 minutes, stirring occasionally, until the sauce is rich and thick and the turkey meat is cooked.

6 Stir in the chopped basil and remove from the heat. Set the Bolognese to one side.

7 Cook the spaghetti according to the packet instructions until al dente.

8 Drain the spaghetti in a colander, and use tongs to lift it into shallow serving bowls. Spoon Bolognese sauce on top of each serving.

9 Sprinkle with plenty of grated Parmesan and add a grind or two more of black pepper before serving.

Peace-Sign Pepper Pasta

Nearly half a million people sure do leave a lot of mess. After the festival was over, some 8,000 volunteers stuck around to help clean up all the crates, plastic, clothes, and other trash left behind. But what I love—LOVE—is that they crafted some of it into a peace sign. Taking garbage and turning it into a symbol of hope and togetherness. It's a great lesson and how I try to live my life. I also try to live my life eating as much pasta as possible.

You will need:

4 chicken breasts, chopped

2 oz (50 g) butter (or canna butter, see page 8, for extra potency)

½ cup (50 g) all-purpose (plain) flour

2 cups (500 ml) canna milk (see page 9)

1 red bell pepper, chopped

1 green bell pepper, chopped

3½ oz (100 g) canned corn kernels

10 oz (300 g) pasta

4 oz (120 g) grated cheese

For the jerk marinade:

5 oz (150 g) chopped onion

1 scotch bonnet or other chili, deseeded and chopped

1 oz (30 g) fresh ginger, peeled and chopped

½ teaspoon ground allspice

a few sprigs of thyme, leaves only

½ teaspoon ground black pepper

5 tablespoons white wine vinegar

5 tablespoons dark soy sauce

Serves 4

1 Put all the marinade ingredients into a food processor and blitz until smooth. Place the chopped chicken breasts in a dish and smother with the marinade. Cover with plastic wrap (cling film) and refrigerate for at least an hour (overnight if you can wait that long).

2 Bring a large pan of water to the boil (this will be for the pasta). Meanwhile, melt the butter in another pan, add the flour, and stir until it forms a smooth paste. Then pour in the canna milk, stirring well with a hand whisk.

3 Put the marinated chicken into a skillet (frying pan) and cook over a medium heat until browned. Add the chopped peppers and corn and continue to cook over a medium heat.

4 Tip the pasta into the boiling water and cook as per the packet's instructions.

5 Meanwhile, slowly bring the sauce to a boil, stirring continuously until it thickens. Remove the pan from the heat and stir in the cheese.

6 When the pasta is ready, the chicken is fully cooked and the peppers are soft, drain the pasta and mix them all together, ready to be served.

Chili Con Candles

Ever wondered where the phenomenon of holding up lighters (now phone screens) whilst swaying at concerts began? Woodstock! Specifically, during Melanie's set. A bunch of candles had been handed out to the crowd beforehand and it wasn't long before we were holding them above our heads, against the pitch-black sky, to display our appreciation. Inspired by this ocean of flickering flames, Melanie went on to write her international-breakthrough hit "Lay Down (Candles in the Rain)." Candlelit chili con carne whilst listening to Melanie's magical music, anyone?

You will need:

2 tablespoons vegetable oil

1 lb (450 g) ground (minced) lean beef

2 white onions, roughly chopped

2 garlic cloves, minced

2 teaspoons chipotle chili powder

1 teaspoon ground cumin

a handful of marijuana, finely chopped

2 tablespoons tomato paste (purée)

1 x 14-oz (400-g) can chopped Italian tomatoes

1 x 14-oz (400-g) can kidney beans, drained and rinsed

1 teaspoon unsweetened cocoa powder

1 beef bouillon (stock) cube

To serve:

rice

sour cream

grated Monterey Jack or cheddar cheese

freshly chopped cilantro (coriander)

Serves 2-3

1 Heat the vegetable oil in a large saucepan. Add the ground (minced) beef and cook for 3-4 minutes until browned. Add the onions and garlic and cook for a further 3-4 minutes until the onions have softened.

2 Add the chipotle chili powder, ground cumin, and marijuana, and stir and cook for 1 minute. Add the tomato paste (purée), canned tomatoes, drained kidney beans, and cocoa powder, and crumble in the bouillon (stock) cube.

3 Add a splash of water, stir, and cook uncovered for about 45 minutes, stirring occasionally and adding a little water if it starts to catch on the bottom of the pan.

4 When ready to serve, cook the rice according to the packet instructions and spoon into deep serving bowls. Spoon in the chili and top with a dollop of sour cream, a sprinkle of grated cheese, and a little chopped cilantro.

Funky Fruity Chicken

"I want to take you higher."

"HIGHER!"

"I want to take you higher."

"HIGHER!"

"I want to take you higher."

"HIGHER!"

In the early hours of Sunday morning, this is what could be heard for miles around. Sly of Sly & The Family Stone whipped us into such a frenzy that we were belting out "HIGHER!" at the top of our lungs and dancing up a storm. The funk-rock band succeeded in taking us higher with the rest of their set too, which included "Dance to the Music" and "Everyday People." Whenever I tuck into my Funky Fruity Chicken, I'm taken higher once again.

You will need:

6 tablespoons vegetable oil

1 white onion, finely chopped

¼ cup (25 g) finely chopped celery

1 garlic clove, minced

4 ready-to-eat soft dried apricots, finely diced

¼ cup (35 g) currants

¼ cup (25 g) pine nuts

1 egg, beaten

8 large chicken thighs

1 heaping teaspoon harissa paste

2 teaspoons runny honey

1 cup (60 g) marijuana, finely chopped

pomegranate seeds, to garnish (optional)

a 12 x 8 x 2-inch (30 x 20 x 5-cm) ovenproof dish, lined with foil

Serves 4–6

1 Preheat the oven to 350°F (180°C) gas 4.

2 Heat 2 tablespoons of the oil in a skillet (frying pan). Add the onion, celery, and garlic. Sauté for about 3 minutes until the onion and celery have softened, but don't allow the garlic to burn.

3 Remove the pan from the heat and add the apricots, currants, pine nuts, and egg. Mix well.

4 Prepare the chicken thighs by pulling the skin away from the meat, without removing it. Stuff the apricot mixture in the cavity between the skin and meat.

5 Arrange the filled chicken pieces in the prepared baking dish.

6 Pour the remaining 4 tablespoons of olive oil into a small dish, add the harissa, honey, and marijuana, and mix together. Brush this mixture over the chicken thighs.

7 Bake the chicken, uncovered, in the preheated oven for 1 hour, basting every 15 minutes, until the thighs are tender.

Chopper Chicken

Due to the horrendous traffic, the organizers of Woodstock had to come up with a Plan B to get bands to the site. Crosby, Stills, Nash & Young, Janis Joplin, Jefferson Airplane, Santana, and Sweetwater were among the bands choppered in. They were all amazed by the sheer size of the audience. Sweetwater's keyboard player Alex Del Zoppo couldn't fathom what they were flying over, so asked the helicopter pilot what kind of crops he was seeing. He laughed and replied, "Those are people, dude."

You will need:

1 whole chicken (about ½ lb/2 kg)

1 lemon, halved

a bunch of thyme

1 stick (115 g) unsalted butter, cut into small pieces

1 cup (60 g) marijuana, finely chopped

10 small waxy potatoes, scrubbed

8 baby carrots, scrubbed (no need to peel)

4 parsnips, scrubbed and quartered

14 oz (300 g) butternut squash flesh, cubed

1 large red onion, quartered

2 tablespoons olive oil

salt and black pepper

Serves 4

1 Preheat the oven to 400°F (200°C) gas 6.

2 Wash the cavity of the chicken under cold water, and pat dry with paper towels. Insert the lemon halves and the thyme sprigs into the cavity.

3 Place the chicken in a roasting pan, dot all over with the pieces of butter and season generously with salt and pepper. Sprinkle over the marijuana.

4 Put the potatoes and other prepared vegetables into a large bowl, drizzle with the olive oil, season generously with salt and pepper, and toss to coat. Tuck them into the roasting pan to surround the chicken.

5 Put the pan in the preheated oven to roast for about 2 hours. To be certain it's cooked through, stick a knife in the thickest part of the thigh and make sure the juices are running clear. If they are pink, return the chicken to the oven until cooked. When it is done, remove from the oven and let rest for 10 minutes before carving.

6 Serve slices of the chicken plated with the roasted vegetables alongside.

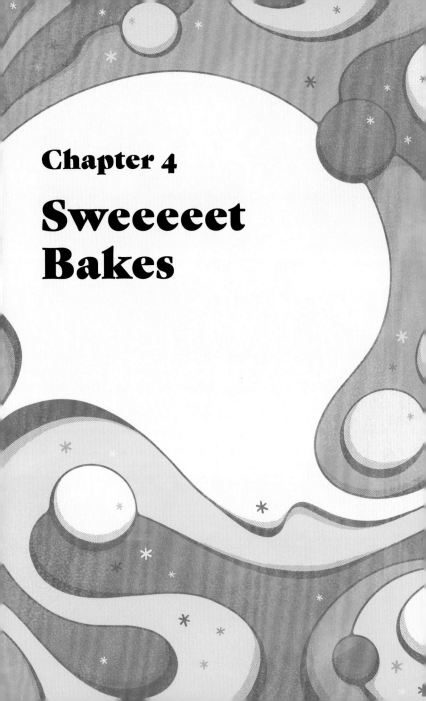

Chapter 4
Sweeeeet Bakes

Canned Heat Cookies

A few years ago, I was watching TV and a GEICO commercial came on. The easy-breezy song it played—"Going Up the Country"—took me right back to Woodstock, seeing Canned Heat perform that very song as the sun set and a night of boogieing ensued. Their other songs brought the crowd pure joy too, and they offered up probably one of the loudest and longest ovations of the entire festival. It's my hope that this delightful combination of salted cashews, sticky caramel, and silky cannabutter brings you just as much joy.

You will need:

4 oz (125 g) cannabutter, softened (see page 8)

½ cup (100 g) soft light brown sugar

½ cup (100 g) superfine (caster) sugar

1 egg, lightly beaten

1 teaspoon vanilla extract

1¾ cups (225 g) all-purpose (plain) flour

2 teaspoons salt

½ teaspoon baking soda (bicarbonate of soda)

3½ oz (100 g) caramels, chopped

3½ oz (100 g) salted cashews, roughly chopped

2 baking sheets, greased

Makes 12-18 cookies

1 Preheat the oven to 350°F (180°C) gas 4.

2 In a bowl, cream together the cannabutter and sugars.

3 Add the egg along with the vanilla. Mix well.

4 Sift in the flour, salt, and baking soda (bicarbonate of soda) and mix together. Add the chopped caramels and cashew nuts to the dough and mix in.

5 Roll the dough into balls about 2 inches (5 cm) wide and flatten slightly onto the baking sheets. Don't pack the cookies too close together as they do spread when cooking.

6 Bake in the oven for 8 minutes for a really gooey cookie or up to 14 minutes for a slightly crisper one. They may seem undercooked, but they will harden considerably as they cool.

Kozmic Cookies

Janis Joplin—bedecked in tie-dyed velvet bell-bottoms and matching blouse—is said to have been so overwhelmed by the size of the crowd that she spent much of the time preceding her performance getting high. Despite not being in the best shape come 2am when she took to the stage with The Kozmic Blues Band, she still rocked the house with her soulful, gutsy voice. I particularly enjoyed the ballad "Kozmic Blues," so named these cookies in its honor. Sweet and a little nutty.

You will need:

½ cup (110 g) smooth peanut butter

6 oz (180 g) cannabutter (see page 8)

1¼ cups (175 g) all-purpose (plain) flour

1 egg, beaten

½ teaspoon vanilla extract

½ teaspoon baking soda (bicarbonate of soda)

½ cup (110 g) brown sugar

¼ teaspoon salt

1 cup (170 g) bittersweet (dark) chocolate chips

½ cup (75 g) salted peanuts, finely chopped

1 tablespoon superfine (caster) sugar

a baking sheet, lined with baking parchment

Makes about 12

1 Preheat the oven to 350°F (180°C) gas 4.

2 Add all the ingredients, except the salted peanuts and superfine (caster) sugar to a bowl and use a wooden spoon to bring the ingredients all together. Tip out onto a board and knead the mixture until it forms a dough.

3 Roll the dough into a cylinder about 3 inches (7.5 cm) in diameter and chill in the fridge for about 20 minutes.

4 Use a sharp knife to slice the cylinder into 1 inch (2.5 cm) thick rounds to create as many cookies as you can. Use a spatula to lift them onto the lined baking sheet.

5 Bake the cookies in the preheated oven for 25 minutes, or until the edges of the cookies are slightly golden.

6 Remove the baking sheet from the oven and sprinkle the top of each cookie with chopped peanuts and sugar, then return them to the oven for a further 5 minutes.

7 At the end of cooking time, remove the cookies from the oven, let cool slightly, and then transfer to a wire rack to cool completely before serving.

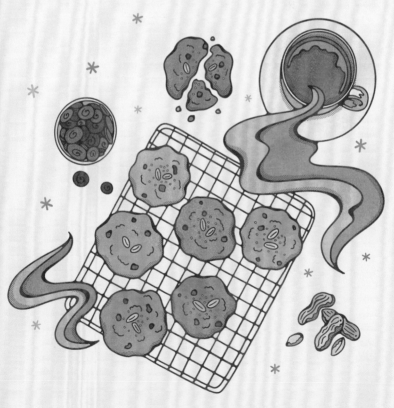

Sha Na Na Shortbread

The award for the most random and out-of-place act at Woodstock had to go to Sha Na Na, the rock 'n' roll cover group who doo-wopped, dit-dit-ditted, and sha-na-na'd their way through the penultimate set of the festival, right before Jimi Hendrix closed. Having been up all night (and most of the two previous days), when the band began belting out '50s classics like "At The Hop," "The Book of Love," and "Get A Job" from around 7.45am on Monday morning, I was as bewildered as the rest of the crowd. But also delighted. The singers' voices were as smooth and moreish as the butter in this shortbread.

You will need:

4 tablespoons unsalted butter, softened

4 tablespoons cannabutter, softened (see page 8)

1¼ cups (175 g) all-purpose (plain) flour

1 tablespoon dried lavender flowers (culinary quality)

2 teaspoons finely grated lemon zest

¼ cup (50 g) superfine (caster) sugar

a round cookie cutter

a baking sheet, lined with baking parchment

Makes about 24

1 Place the butter, cannabutter, and sugar in a mixing bowl and cream together using a wooden spoon until thoroughly combined and pale.

2 Sift in the flour and add the lavender flowers and lemon zest. Use a wooden spoon to mix until you have a smooth mixture with a dough-like consistency.

3 Place the dough on a clean work surface and use a rolling pin to roll it out until it's about ½ inch (1.5 cm) thick.

4 Use the cookie cutter to stamp out about 24 rounds of dough. Sprinkle each one with a little sugar.

5 Place on the prepared baking sheet and chill in the refrigerator for 20 minutes. Meanwhile, preheat the oven to 375°F (180ºC) gas 5.

6 Bake in the preheated oven for 15–20 minutes until the shortbread is a pale golden color.

7 Leave to cool on a wire rack before serving.

Joni Mitchell 'Jacks

Although Joni didn't actually make it to the festival (damn you, scheduling issues), she wrote the beautiful "Woodstock" from her New York hotel room as she watched it on TV. As I've been melting, stirring, and chopping to prepare these delicious flapjacks, I must have listened to the track about a hundred times. It never gets old. I've been belting it out at the top of my lungs (sorry John next door) and even had a little cry, such is the beauty of Joni's pure voice. As I dusted the sugar on top, singing, "We are stardust, we are golden," I got chills.

You will need:

6 tablespoons unsalted butter, softened

4 tablespoons cannabutter, softened (see page 8)

¼ cup (50 g) white granulated sugar

¼ cup (60 ml) clear honey

2 cups (200 g) old-fashioned rolled (porridge) oats

Ginger frosting:

¾ cup (175 g) unsalted butter

1¾ cups (200 g) confectioners' (icing) sugar, plus extra for dusting

4 tablespoons corn (golden) syrup

2 tablespoons ground ginger

a few chunks of crystallized ginger

a brownie pan, greased and lined with baking parchment

Makes 9–12

1 Preheat the oven to 400°F (200°C) gas 6.

2 To make the flapjack base, put the butter, cannabutter, sugar, honey, and oats in a mixing bowl. Use a wooden spoon to mix thoroughly until well combined.

3 Spoon the mixture into the prepared brownie pan and use the back of a large metal spoon to level the surface.

4 Bake the flapjack in the preheated oven for about 10 minutes.

5 Remove the flapjack from the oven and set aside to cool in the pan.

6 Meanwhile, make the frosting. Put the butter, sugar, syrup, and ground ginger in a small saucepan and heat until melted. Pour this mixture over the cooled flapjack in the pan and scatter with pieces of crystallized ginger. Let cool in the pan before cutting into pieces.

7 Dust with a little confectioners' (icing) sugar to serve.

Dove Donuts

I have a framed Woodstock poster hanging in my bedroom.
On it, the slogan "3 Days of Peace & Music" sits below
a guitar neck with a white bird perched on top. I always
assumed—as did the rest of the world—that the bird was a
dove (the symbol of peace and love) but I recently learned
that the artist who designed the logo, Arnold Skolnick, took
inspiration from a catbird. Regardless, I named these little
bites of heaven Dove Donuts, and I know they'll leave your
taste buds all aflutter.

You will need:

2 cups (250 g) all-purpose
(plain) flour

1½ cups (300 g) superfine
(caster) sugar

2 teaspoons baking powder

1 teaspoon ground cinnamon

½ teaspoon ground nutmeg

½ teaspoon salt

1 oz (30 g) cannabutter (see page 8)

1 large (UK medium) egg

1¼ cups (300 ml) full-fat (whole)
milk

2 teaspoons vanilla extract

For the coating:

½ cup (100 g) superfine (caster)
sugar

½ teaspoon ground cinnamon

4 oz (120 g) cannabutter (see page 8)

2 x 6-hole donut pans, well greased

Makes 12

1 Preheat the oven to 350°F (180°C) gas 4.

2 Sift the dry ingredients together into a mixing bowl.

3 Melt the cannabutter in another bowl in a microwave, and
then add the egg, milk, and vanilla. Then whisk it all together.
Pour this mixture into the dry ingredients and stir until it's
all combined.

4 Pour the batter into the donut pans so each hole is about
three-quarters full. Bake in the oven for 15–20 minutes. The
donuts are ready when you poke them with a knife and it
comes out clean.

5 While the donuts are cooling, make the coating. Mix the sugar and cinnamon together in a bowl, then melt the cannabutter in a pan.

6 Dunk each donut in the melted cannabutter and roll it in the sugar and cinnamon.

Trippy Brownies

Weed wasn't the only drug at Woodstock; acid was also free-flowing. Grace Slick of Jefferson Airplane referred to their stash as "orange," while an announcement was made to the crowd warning them to steer clear of the "brown acid" as it was "not specifically too good." Whilst you won't find any LSD in these delicious orange and cranberry brownies, one bite and you'll be tripping over yourself for more.

You will need:

½ cup (55 g) self-rising (self-raising) flour

½ teaspoon baking powder

⅓ cup (40 g) unsweetened cocoa powder

¼ cup (25 g) ground almonds

1 cup (225 g) soft brown sugar

finely grated zest of 1 large unwaxed orange

4½ oz (120 g) cannabutter (see page 8)

2 eggs, lightly beaten

2 heaped tablespoons dried cranberries

a brownie pan, greased and lined with baking parchment

Makes 16

1 Preheat the oven to 300°F (150°C) gas 2.

2 Sift the flour, baking powder, and cocoa powder into a large mixing bowl.

3 Add the ground almonds, sugar, and grated orange zest, and thoroughly mix together using a wooden spoon.

4 Add the cannabutter and eggs, and then vigorously beat the mixture until smooth. Fold in the cranberries.

5 Spoon the mixture into the prepared brownie pan and use a spatula to level the surface. Bake in the preheated oven for about 45–50 minutes. The brownies are done when a skewer inserted in the middle comes out clean.

6 Leave to cool in the pan and then tip the brownie onto a wooden board and peel off the baking parchment. Use a serrated knife to cut into 16 squares to serve.

Schmuck S'mores

When I recently watched the 1970 *Woodstock* documentary (again!), it called for an accompanying snack that was sweet, decadent, and delicious. Enter the Schmuck S'mores, so-named after the legendary director Martin Scorsese, who cut his chops as assistant director and editor on the film. In an interview for *Rolling Stone* magazine, cameraman Hart Perry said of his young colleague: "He wasn't Martin Scorsese yet, he was just some schmuck from Little Italy." This "schmuck" and the rest of the crew could never have imagined that their 120 hours of raw footage would transform into an Oscar.

You will need:

1 jar chocolate and hazelnut spread, such as Nutella

20 Graham crackers (digestive biscuits)

1 cup (60 g) finely chopped marijuana leaves

40–50 mini marshmallows

Makes 10

1 Preheat the oven to 325°F (170°C) gas 3.

2 Spread a generous helping of chocolate and hazelnut spread onto all the crackers (biscuits). Sprinkle a little chopped marijuana on top of each.

3 Add 4–5 mini marshmallows to 10 of the chocolate and hazelnut spread-topped crackers.

4 Pair the crackers together to make 10 sandwich cookies, each filled with the spread, marijuana, and marshmallows.

5 Place the sandwich cookies on a baking sheet and cook in the preheated oven for 15 minutes, until the marshmallows have melted.

6 Serve immediately, while the filling is still gooey.

Sweeter-Than-Ever Brownies

Although shouts of "Where's Dylan?" were hurled at the stage during The Band's set, I was too captivated by the melodic music to worry that the man himself wasn't there. Bob Dylan's former backing band were rocking out on their own, putting on one helluva show, with songs like "The Weight" (featured in *Easy Rider*, released the same year as Woodstock), and "Loving You is Sweeter Than Ever." You know what else is sweeter than ever? These moreish marshmallow brownies! As a nod to The Band's album, *Music from Big Pink* ("Big Pink" was the blush-colored house where they wrote their songs), I use pink marshmallows.

You will need:

2 cups (400 g) superfine (caster) sugar

8 oz (225 g) cannabutter, melted (see page 8)

½ cup (60 g) unsweetened cocoa powder

1 teaspoon vanilla extract

4 eggs, lightly beaten

1¾ cups (225 g) all-purpose (plain) flour

½ teaspoon baking powder

½ cup (100 g) white chocolate chunks

7 oz (200 g) mini marshmallows

½ cup (100 g) milk chocolate chips

a 9 x 13-inch (23 x 33-cm) brownie pan, greased and lined with baking parchment

Makes 18

1 Preheat the oven to 350°F (180°C) gas 4.

2 In a large bowl, cream together the sugar, cannabutter, cocoa powder, and vanilla. Add the eggs.

3 Sift in the flour and baking powder and mix thoroughly.

4 When mixed, stir in the white chocolate chunks. Make the chunks reasonably large so they don't melt away in the oven.

5 Pour the mixture into the lined pan, spreading it into the corners. Bake for 25–30 minutes until the top looks cooked.

6 Remove from the oven and cover the top of the brownie with a blanket of marshmallows, then sprinkle the milk chocolate chips on top.

7 Return to the oven for a few minutes so the marshmallows melt slightly and begin to turn brown.

8 It will be really hot and sticky, so resist the temptation to dive straight in; instead leave it to cool fully before taking out of the pan and cutting into 18 squares.

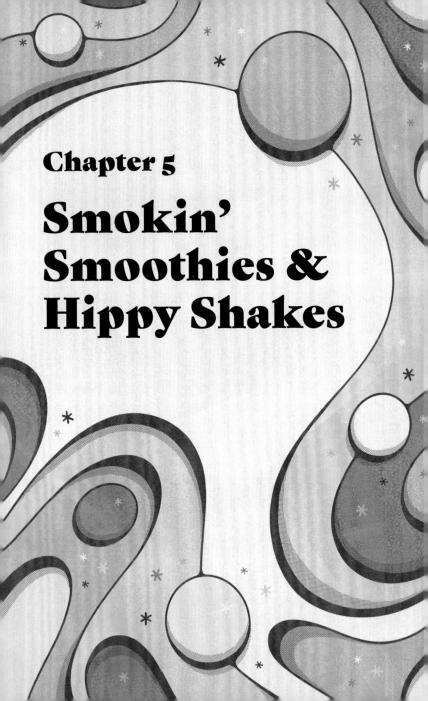

Chapter 5

Smokin' Smoothies & Hippy Shakes

Sun-Upper Smoothies

You've heard of sundowner cocktails; these are sun-upper smoothies, inspired by The Who's "See Me, Feel Me." As they were singing this beautiful tune on Sunday morning, the sun rose as if on cue... and I thought my heart might just burst with happiness. Bassist John Entwistle later said, "God was our lighting man."

Banana, Kiwi & Ginger Smoothie

You will need:

1 cup (250 ml) canna milk (see page 9)

1 banana, sliced

1 kiwi fruit

a handful of ice cubes

1 tablespoon honey

1 teaspoon vanilla extract

1-inch (2.5-cm) piece ginger, finely grated

Serves 2

Strawberry & Cinnamon Smoothie

You will need:

1 cup (250 ml) canna milk (see page 9)

1 banana, sliced

5 strawberries

a handful of ice cubes

1–2 teaspoons ground cinnamon

Serves 2

To make these delicious drinks, simply whiz all the ingredients together in a blender.

Muddy Milkshakes

Boy, did it rain! I lost my sandals in the mud at some point on the second day... but was I about to let the deluge dampen my spirit? Hell, no! As you sip these Muddy Milkshakes, imagine yourself—raindrops on your eyelids, hair slick, surrounded by comrades—as you slip and slide in time to the magical music. The downpour of rain only added to the outpouring of love.

Quadruple Chocolate Milkshake

You will need:

1 cup (250 ml) canna milk (see page 9)

2 tablespoons chocolate syrup

1 tablespoon unsweetened cocoa powder

1 pint (500 ml) chocolate ice cream

your favorite chocolate bar, chopped into pieces

Serves 2

Cookies and Cream Milkshake

You will need:

1 cup (250 ml) canna milk (see page 9)

1 pint (500 ml) vanilla ice cream

1 teaspoon vanilla extract

8 Oreo cookies, broken into pieces

Serves 2

To make these delicious drinks, simply whiz all the ingredients together in a blender.

Rainbow Shake

John Sebastian (of The Lovin' Spoonful fame) wasn't even supposed to play at Woodstock. But I'm so glad he did. As I'm sure the parents of the baby who had just been born were when he dedicated "Younger Generation" to them, saying, "Whew, that kid's gonna be far out."

You will need:

4 ripe bananas

a handful of strawberries

a sprinkle of hash

a sprinkle of honey

2½ cups (600 ml) milk

1¼ cups (300 ml) light (single) cream

½ cup (120 ml) Green River (see page 60)

Serves 4

1 Throw the bananas and strawberries into a blender. Sprinkle in some hash and honey.

2 Whiz everything to a pulp.

3 Add the milk, cream, and Green River. Blend again until the whole thing is bubbling. Put into the refrigerator for an hour, and serve cool.

Green River

My take on "green dragon"—the cannabis-infused liquor—
Green River is inspired by Creedence Clearwater Revival's
song of the same name. Performing it second in their
Woodstock set, I later found out that it was based on
a childhood vacation spot of frontman John Fogerty's,
and named after his favorite soda pop syrup flavor (lime).
The band's performance of "I Put a Spell on You" also caught
my attention. This powerful potation, which sees the THC
extracted from the marijuana, will certainly leave you
spellbound... and stoned.

Basic recipe:

1 Look out for a bottle of natural-grain alcohol. It's hard
to come by, so grab more than one bottle if you find some.
Use the highest-proof alcohol you can find (if you can get it,
190-proof is highly recommended).

2 Score the best-quality dope you can find. Use about
½ gram of dope per 1 fl oz (30 ml) of alcohol.

3 Break up the marijuana and take out the seeds. You can
also use the stems.

4 Crack open the bottle of alcohol and pour about one-
quarter of it away, so there's room for the weed. Carefully
add the broken-up dope plant into the bottle. Put the cap
back on the bottle and shake.

5 Store the bottle in a safe place (away from sunlight) and
let it work its magic for about 2–3 weeks. As the weeks
progress, you'll find the solution begins to take on
a green tint (hence the name).

6 After the 2–3 weeks are up, pour the green-tinted mixture
into another container through a strainer, such as a coffee
filter or cheesecloth (muslin).

7 The result is a high-proof alcohol-laced solution with large
amounts of pure THC.

Green River Spritz

1 Mix 3 parts of 7-Up or cola with 1 part Green River. Stir in a spoonful of honey.

2 Serve in a highball glass with ice.

Sundown Cocktail

1 Get a tall glass. Fill it one-quarter full with Green River. Top it up to half with rum.

2 Then hit the brim with a mix of freshly squeezed orange juice and pomegranate juice.

3 If you don't own a cocktail shaker, just use a regular bottle and shake vigorously. Drop in some ice for that extra finishing touch.

Blissful Bhang

Described by his good friend George Harrison as "the godfather of world music," Indian sitar maestro Ravi Shankar didn't let the heavy wind and rain during his Woodstock set dampen his spirits. And the crowd didn't either; drenched in rain and enlightenment, we were thrilled to watch the man who had inspired the likes of The Beatles, The Byrds, and The Rolling Stones to incorporate an Eastern element into their own music. Mix yourself this drink, blended with warming Indian spice mix garam masala, and allow your mind to drift away as you listen to Shankar's soothing sounds.

You will need:

1 oz (25 g) marijuana

2 cups (475 ml) boiling water

4 cups (950 ml) warm milk

2 tablespoons blanched and chopped almonds

⅛ teaspoon garam masala

¼ teaspoon ground ginger

½–1 teaspoon rosewater

1 cup (200 g) sugar

Serves 6–8

1 Remove any seeds or twigs from the marijuana, and place the leaves and flowers in a teapot. Pour on the boiling water. Put the teapot lid on and let the infusion brew for about 10 minutes.

2 Strain the marijuana water through a tea strainer or cheesecloth (muslin), and put the water to one side.

3 Take the leaves and flowers left in the strainer and squeeze out any excess water into the marijuana water.

4 Place the leaves and flowers in a mortar and add 2 teaspoons of the warm milk. Using a pestle, slowly and firmly grind the milk and leaves together.

5 Gather up the leaves and flowers and squeeze out as much milk as you can into a bowl.

6 Repeat this process until you have used about ½ cup (120 ml) of milk. By this stage the marijuana should have turned into a pulp.

7 Add the chopped almonds and some more warm milk to the marijuana pulp. Grind this in the mortar until it becomes a sticky paste. Squeeze the paste and collect the extract as before in a bowl. Repeat a few more times until all that is left are some fibers and nut meal. Throw away what's left.

8 Combine the marijuana water and milk, the garam masala, ginger, and rosewater. Add the sugar and remaining milk.

9 Chill in the refrigerator for a few hours. Serve cool and hit the stars!

Cup of Joe

I didn't just see and hear Joe Cocker perform—I *felt* him. What. A. Performance. Dare I be so bold as to say he sang The Beatles classic "With a Little Help from My Friends" better than the Fab Four? As I pour this cannabis-laced Cup of Joe, I recall him pouring his heart, soul and guts into that song. His impassioned rendition of "Let's Go Get Stoned"— which I took as a call to action—was also a highlight.

You will need:

1 heaped teaspoon finely powdered Arabian mocha

a small pinch of ground cardamom

½ g pulverized hashish

1 pot good-quality coffee

1 teaspoon honey

Serves 4–6

1 Place the mocha, cardamom, and hashish in a Turkish coffee pot. Pour on the coffee. Heat the Turkish pot over a low heat until it begins to bubble, then take it off the heat immediately.

2 Serve in espresso cups with a small spoon. Dissolve in the honey. Sip the coffee, and then scoop up whatever is left with the spoon.

Index